Science Action Labs
Astronomy

Written by Ed Shevick

Illustrated by Mary Galan Rojas

Teaching & Learning Company

1204 Buchanan St., P.O. Box 10
Carthage, IL 62321-0010

This book belongs to

_____

Cover art by Mary Galan Rojas

Copyright © 2002, Teaching & Learning Company

ISBN No. 1-57310-362-4

Printing No. 987654321

Teaching & Learning Company
1204 Buchanan St., P.O. Box 10
Carthage, IL 62321-0010

Table of Contents
Science Action Labs

Dear Teacher or Parent,

Welcome to *Science Action Labs: Astronomy*. This book is built around solid scientific concepts which are backed up by basic facts. The concepts are made real by meaningful activities and experiments designed to interest and motivate your children. Each one involves some part of the scientific process. All activities are not suitable for every age or ability. This gives the teacher an opportunity to pick and choose for particular children.

Since the concepts build on one another, proceed from lab 1 onward. However, each chapter can stand on its own as an independent lab if you choose to teach them in a different order.

Sometimes it may be best to do the activities as demonstrations instead of lab activities. Questions are provided for group discussions.

Above all, children should be allowed to enjoy science. Fun and excitement are inherent in the process of discovery. To make the fact-finding activities in this study more fun, meet C.D. (collecting data), his ally Allie and her cat Orbit. They'll help children gather and process information and encourage them as only kids can do.

Sincerely,

Ed

Ed Shevick

The Universe

Astronomy

1

Myths About the Universe

What is the universe? You and your family are part of it. Our Earth and moon are only a small part of it. The universe includes the sun and all the planets. It includes all the stars and the dust and space that reaches beyond our imagination.

People have always had myths about the universe. Myths are tales that explain the unknown. One myth told that the universe hatched from a giant egg. Another myth said the universe was created by giants. An Egyptian myth had the gods giving birth to the Earth and stars.

Not so long ago some people claimed to see a "man" in the moon. Others saw "canals" on Mars and thought that meant water and life. Scientists now believe there is no life or water on Mars.

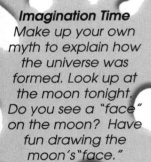

Imagination Time
Make up your own myth to explain how the universe was formed. Look up at the moon tonight. Do you see a "face" on the moon? Have fun drawing the moon's "face."

Facts About the Universe

How old are you? How old is your grandfather? How old is the universe? The best guess is that the universe is 15 to 20 billion years old. Can you count to a billion?

How far away from home is your school? How far away is the edge of the universe? Would you like to take a spaceship to the nearest planet? The trip could take three months. If you went to the farthest planet, it would take you 60 years. You would be a senior citizen by then.

The Universe

Let's say your spaceship could move with the speed of light. Light is so fast, it can circle the Earth almost eight times in one second. If you could ride a light beam, it would still take four years to reach the nearest star. It would take 10 billion years to reach the farthest star.

How was the universe formed? People have different ideas about how it all began. The big bang theory says that all matter in the universe was packed into a small, dense ball. An explosion blew all the matter outward to form the stars and planets. Some scientists say the universe is still expanding.

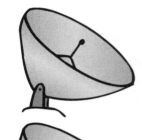

 ## Life in the Universe

The Earth is a great planet for life. It has water, air and the right temperature. Is there life somewhere else in the universe? Nobody knows for sure.

Does life elsewhere in the universe have to look and live like us? No, life could take many forms. Could living creatures in the universe be as intelligent as we are? Could they be more intelligent? What do you think?

Is there life on distant stars? Probably not; star temperatures seem much too high to support life. But there could be planets around stars that have the air, water and temperature to support life.

Planet Earth circles our star, the sun. There are probably millions of planets circling stars in our universe.

For many years we have been listening for radio messages from our universe. So far we have heard nothing. For many years we have been sending radio messages into space. We have sent music, maps and symbols. We are still waiting for an answer.

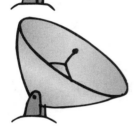

Hello! Is there anyone out there?

6

Making Contact

You have just been appointed the Earth's top scientist. What drawings, photos or symbols will you send to intelligent beings in space? Write or draw your best ideas in the boxes.

Rocket into the Universe

To explore the universe, you will need a rocket ship. Here is a simple one that you can make. It will get you the first two feet above Earth! You will need a plastic squeeze bottle and some straws.

1. Fold a 2" section of straw as shown in the sketch. Tape it so that it is airtight.
2. Place the other end of the straw on the bottle tip as shown.
3. Squeeze the bottle quickly to launch your rocket. With practice, you'll soon be able to launch it higher.
4. Try using different straws. Try using half a straw.
5. Give your rocket a name. Compete with friends to launch the highest rocket.

Universe Word Contest

Universe is an eight-letter word. How many words can you make using only the eight letters in the word? You can use "E" twice and the other letters once.

1. _____
2. _____
3. _____
4. _____
5. _____

6. _____
7. _____
8. _____
9. _____
10. _____

8

Astronauts in Space

Astronomy 2

Why Go into Space?

Life is an adventure. Some people climb mountains. Some dive deep into the ocean.

Some people think the biggest adventure is going into space. Would you want to step on the moon? Would you like to spend some time circling the Earth in a spaceship?

Space travel is an expensive adventure. It costs billions of dollars to explore space. But it has brought about some amazing discoveries. Here is a list of some benefits that have come out of our space adventure.

1. Television by satellite
2. Telephones by satellite
3. Satellite weather stations
4. Satellites that can find oil and coal deposits on Earth
5. Space labs that discover new medicines and materials
6. G.P.S. navigation (*G.P.S.* means "Global Positioning System.") Using a telephone sized device, you can pinpoint your exact location anywhere on Earth.

Describe three situations when G.P.S. would be useful to people.

1. _____

2. _____

3. _____

For every dollar spent on space programs, we have discovered $8 of new products.

Astronauts in Space

The History of Space Travel

Here is a brief summary of some adventures in space.

1957: Russians launch *Sputnik,* a small unmanned ball that sends radio signals back to Earth.
1961: Russian Yuri Gagarin becomes the first man in space.
1964: American John Glenn flies three orbits around the Earth.
1965: American spacecraft *Gemini 7* spends 14 days in orbit.
1969: American Neil Armstrong lands on the moon.
1973: American *Sky Lab* placed in orbit to carry on space experiments.
1981: American space shuttle used to travel back and forth in space.
1998: International space station launched. Planned and built by many nations. Space shuttles are now taking up parts for a new space station. It will be completed in 2004.

When Neil Armstrong stepped on the moon, he said these words: "One small step for a man, one giant leap for mankind."

Imagination Time
What would you have said if you were the first person on the moon?

Astronauts in Space

Astronauts Tests

Astronauts are picked for their physical and mental ability. They receive years of training.

Following are some astronaut tests you can try on your friends.

CLAP!

Hearing Test

Have a friend sit on a chair with eyes closed. Snap your fingers or click something above, below or behind your friend. How many times in five tries can he or she point to the sound?

Memory Test

Say five simple words such as *dog, cat, cow, lion* or *tiger*. Say the words just once. Can your friend repeat the words backwards?

Finger Touch Test

Have a friend stand with his or her eyes closed and try to touch two fingers together in front of his or her face. Then carefully spin him or her around five times and repeat the test.

Reactions Speed Test

Have a friend sit on a chair with his or her right shoe stretched forward. Drop a lightweight ball from above your friend's head towards the shoe. Drop the ball from different spots, not directly above the shoe. The future astronaut must move his or her foot so the ball hits the shoe.

11

Space Quiz

Circle *true* or *false* for each statement.

1. Neil Armstrong was the first man to step on Mars.
   True or False?

2. America launched *Sputnik* in 1957.
   True or False?

3. *G.P.S.* stands for "Great Pluto Spaceship."
   True or False?

4. Space satellites can help us phone a friend.
   True or False?

5. All astronauts are pilots.
   True or False?

6. Astronauts must be in top physical condition.
   True or False?

7. Only Americans are building the space station.
   True or False?

8. Space satellites can find oil and coal deposits on Earth.
   True or False?

Our Home Called Earth

Astronomy

3

The Great Planet

Imagine that you are on a spaceship somewhere in the universe. You are looking for a suitable place to live.

You pass groups of stars called **galaxies**. One galaxy catches your eye. It is the **Milky Way** galaxy.

You glide through the Milky Way galaxy until you see the **sun**. It has **nine planets** circling it.

You spot a reddish planet called **Mars**. It is too cold for life. You see a planet called **Venus**. It is too hot for life.

Then you see a blue planet called **Earth**. The blue color is due to the oceans of water. The temperature is perfect for life.

You land on Earth. It has plenty of water for life. The air has oxygen for breathing. Plants and animals provide plenty of food. Inside Earth are coal and oil for energy.

Earth has everything that life needs. However, even Earth could be improved. List four ways that you think Earth could be improved.

1. _____

2. _____

3. _____

4. _____

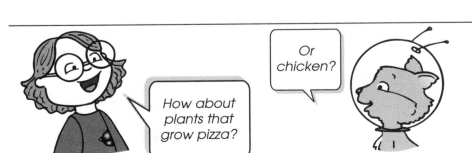

How about plants that grow pizza?

Or chicken?

Our Home Called Earth

The Size and Shape of the Earth

The Earth is round like a ball. Ancient people thought the Earth was flat. They were afraid that a ship could sail too far and fall off the Earth!

Look around. The Earth does look flat, even from the top of a mountain. How do we know the Earth is really round?

Here are four good proofs:

1. You can see the roundness of the Earth from space or even from a high-flying plane.
2. All the other planets are round.
3. Think of a ship sailing into the distance. If the Earth were flat, the ship would just get smaller and smaller. Instead, the last thing you see is the mast as it sinks behind the curved Earth.
4. The Earth casts a round shadow during an eclipse.

A trip through the Earth is about 8000 miles. A trip around the Earth is about 25,000 miles.

The Earth is not a perfectly round ball. It is slightly fatter at the equator than it is at the poles. The difference is only about 25 miles. The bulge at the equator is due to the Earth's rotation.

The Earth rotates (spins) once every 24 hours. At the equator the Earth is moving 1000 miles an hour. This fast rotation bulges the Earth outward.

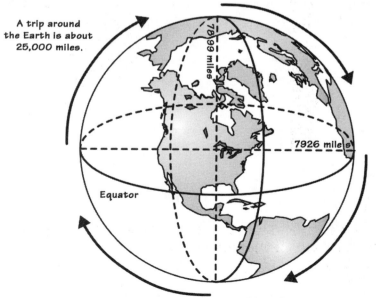

A trip around the Earth is about 25,000 miles.

7899 miles

7926 miles

Equator

14

TLC10362 Copyright © Teaching & Learning Company, Carthage, IL 62321-0010

An Experiment with Rotation

Here is a rotating gadget you can make. It will show you how the Earth bulges.

1. Cut a strip 12" long and 1¹/₂" wide from heavy paper.
2. Form the strip into a circle and tape the ends together.
3. Use a thumbtack to tightly pin your paper circle to the eraser of a pencil as shown.
4. Rotate (spin) the pencil between the palms of your hands.

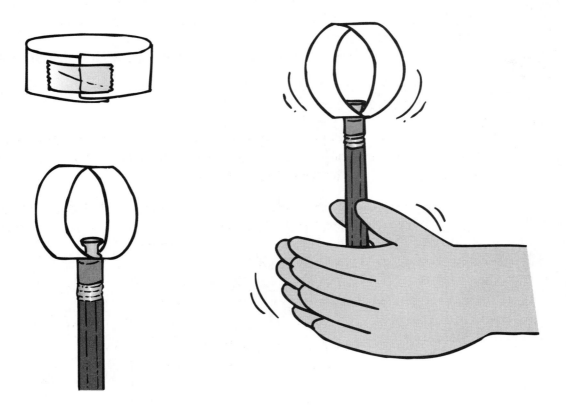

Did your paper circle bulge outward as it was rotated? What causes the Earth to bulge at the equator?

Our Home Called Earth

The Earth in Motion

Here is a way to demonstrate the Earth's rotation and revolution.

1. Find a large globe of the Earth or use a basketball to represent the Earth.
2. Remove the shade from a floor lamp. Place the lamp in the center of a dark room and turn the light on to represent the sun.
3. Stand a short distance from the light. Slowly rotate the Earth globe in a complete circle. This would be a 24-hour day.
4. Walk in a complete circle around the light. This represents a year with 365 days.
5. Now combine the two movements. As you revolve around the sun, rotate the globe. If your globe were the Earth, it would make 365 globe rotations as you made the yearly revolution.

The Earth rotates or spins on its axis.

The Earth revolves around the sun.

And I just sit here and don't even feel dizzy!

Celebrate!
You love birthdays. When you were born, the Earth and the sun were in a certain position. Your birthday occurs when a year passes and the Earth and sun are in the same position.

16

Our Home Called Earth

Why Doesn't Earth Fly off into Space?

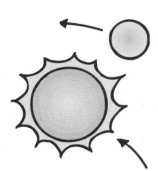

You may have traveled 70 miles an hour in a car or 700 miles an hour in an airplane. You and the Earth are now traveling 70,000 miles an hour on your trip together around the sun.

Why doesn't the Earth fly off into space at that speed? Sir Isaac Newton was a famous scientist who gave us the answer.

The Earth is balanced between two forces. One force is the 70,000 mile-per-hour speed. The other force is the pull of the sun's gravity. They balance and the Earth stays in orbit.

A Demonstration of Speed and Gravity

Here is a way to demonstrate speed and gravity.

1. Find a light, plastic pail. Tie two feet of strong rope to the pail's handle.
2. Fill the pail one-fourth full of water.
3. Go outside to a safe place. Keep your friends at a safe distance.
4. Rotate the pail of water rapidly in front of you.

The water did not fall out even when the pail was upside down, did it? The speed of rotation forced it to the bottom of the pail.

The rope is the other force that keeps the pail from flying into space. It acts like the sun's gravity.

17

Earth Friendly Quiz

1. What is the difference between the Earth's rotation and revolution?

   _____

   _____

   _____

2. What force from the sun keeps the Earth in orbit?

   _____

3. Unscramble these five words. They are things that make life on Earth possible.

   A. terwa   B. thea   C. ira   D. dofo   E. ergyen

   _____   _____   _____   _____   _____

4. Arrange these according to size with the largest first:

   moon   galaxy   solar system   universe   Earth

5. Scientists have discovered "proofs" that tell us the Earth is round like a ball. Can you make up a "proof" that the Earth is flat?

   _____

   _____

   _____

   _____

   _____

The Sun

Sun Questions

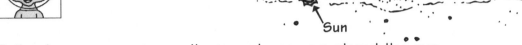

Sun

Following are some questions and answers about the sun.

1. Where is our sun located in space?

   The sun is only one of millions of stars located in the Milky Way galaxy. The sun is halfway out in one of the spiral arms.

2. How old is the sun?

   Most scientists believe the sun is almost five billion years old. It will probably last another five billion years before it burns out.

3. How big is the sun?

   The sun is not the biggest star in the universe, but it is still huge. Over a million Earths would fit inside the sun.

4. How far away is the sun?

   The sun is 93 million miles away from Earth. If you were driving a car at 50 miles an hour, it would take you about 200 years to get to the sun.

5. How hot is the sun?

   A comfortable temperature is 70°F. Your body stays below 100°F. You would not be happy on the sun. The sun's surface is about 10,000°F. An iron nail would boil on the sun.

Sun Fun
Use three-letter words to describe the sun. You are given the first letter. Can you guess the other two?

1. H _ _
2. F _ _
3. B _ _
4. O _ _

The Sun

A Trip to the Sun

Let's take an imaginary trip to the sun. We couldn't really get near the sun without burning up.

First we reach the sun's **corona**. This is an area of hot gasses surrounding the sun.

Next we enter the **chromosphere**. It also is made of hot gas that flares outward from the sun's surface.

The actual surface of the sun is called the **photosphere**. It also is made of hot gasses.

The center of the sun is made of **helium** gas. This is the same gas we use to blow up balloons.

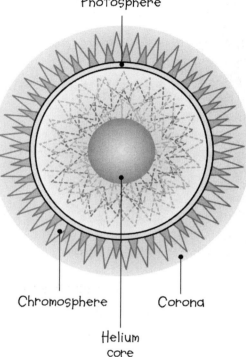

Inside the Sun

Photosphere

Chromosphere

Corona

Helium core

One last observation on our sun trip: There are **sunspots** on the sun's surface. Sunspots are cooler areas on the sun. Some are bigger than the Earth. Sunspots move around on the sun.

Caution! *Never look directly at the sun. Your eyes can be harmed by its brightness,* **even** *if you wear sunglasses.*

Experiment

Here is a safe way to view the sun and maybe see a sunspot.

1 Use a fine needle to poke a pinhole in the *center* of an index card.
2. Go out into the sunlight. You should be facing the cards with your back to the sun. **Remember not to look into the sun.** Hold a second index card beneath the card with the hole in it. The sunlight should pass through the pinhole onto the second card.
3. Move the second card to focus the sun's image.

20

The Sun

Energy from the Sun

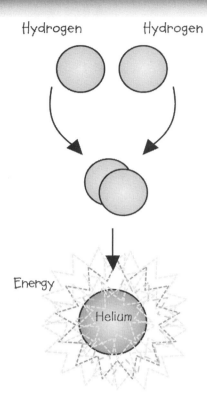

Hydrogen   Hydrogen

Energy

Helium

The sun is a boiling mass of hot gasses. The inside temperature can be 10 million°F.

The source of the sun's energy is an atom called **hydrogen**. The sun is 70% hydrogen.

The high temperatures cause two atoms of hydrogen to join together. They make a new atom called **helium**. Huge amounts of energy are released.

Only a very small amount of the sun's energy reaches the Earth. It is just the right amount for life. Any more, and we would burn up. Any less, and we would freeze.

Experiment

Here is an experiment that shows how the sun heats the Earth.

1. Find a thermometer, a small food can, some black paper and tape.
2. Remove the can's label.
3. Cover the sides of the can with black paper. Tape the black paper tightly to the can.
4. Fill the can half full of water from a faucet.
5. Take the temperature of the water. Write it down.
6. Remove the thermometer and place the can in the bright sun for a half an hour.
7. Take the water temperature again. Write it down.
8. How many degrees did the water temperature rise?
9. What energy source heated the water?

Caution!
Have an adult make sure the edges of the can are smooth.

Black absorbs more of the sun's energy.

The energy found in oil, gas and coal is really trapped sunlight. Can you find out how oil, gas and coal were formed?

Health Hint!
The sun is our friend. It gives us the energy for life. Too much sun can be harmful to your skin. Protect yourself with sunscreen even on cloudy days.

water - - - - - - - - -

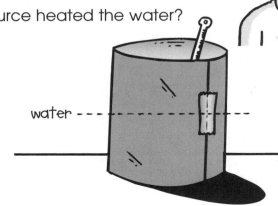

21

Sunny Quiz

Match each sentence with the correct number.

1. Age of the sun
2. Number of Earths that would fit into the sun
3. Temperature in degrees Fahrenheit of the sun's surface
4. Temperature in degrees Fahrenheit of the sun's interior
5. Number of hydrogen atoms needed to make one helium atom
6. Distance from the Earth to the sun
7. Percent of the sun that is hydrogen

A. 70

B. 10,000

C. 1 million

D. 5 billion

E. 93 million

F. 2

G. 10 million

The sun has a **chromosphere** and a **photosphere**. Sphere means "round body." Can you find out what chromo and photo mean?

The Moon: Earth's Nearest Neighbor

Astronomy 5

Moon Superstitions

The moon is the brightest object in the night sky.

Ancient people worshiped the moon as a god. The Romans called their moon goddess Diana. The moon was considered a wonder because it gave light on dark nights.

Actually the moon doesn't give off any light of its own. The light you see is really reflected sunlight.

Native Americans were among some of the ancient people who used the moon to tell the season. They farmed and hunted according to moon cycles.

The moon has a four-week cycle. The original word for *month* was *moonth*.

The Latin name for the moon is luna. That is part of the word *lunatic*, which is a word for someone who acts crazy. Many superstitions said people did crazy things during the full moon.

Superstitions are beliefs based upon fear or ignorance, not facts.

Imagination Time
Make up your own superstition about the moon. It can be funny or scary.

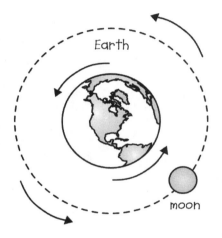

Four-week orbit around the Earth.

The Origin of the Moon

Scientists tell us that the moon travels with the Earth on its yearly trip around the sun. The moon circles the Earth in about four weeks. The moon is about the same age as the Earth. Rocks brought back from the moon are much like Earth rocks.

Here are three theories about how the moon originated:

1. A huge object smashed into the Earth. Matter splashed out of the Earth that eventually formed the moon.
2. The Earth and moon were formed at the same time from matter drifting in space.
3. The moon was formed somewhere in outer space. It drifted near the Earth and was captured by gravity.

Most scientists like theory number 1. It seems to explain the similar ages and rocks best.

The Moon: Earth's Nearest Neighbor

The Size of the Moon

Our beautiful moon is not the only moon in the solar system. **Ganymede** is a moon that circles the planet Jupiter. It is bigger than our moon. Saturn has a moon that is less than 60 miles in diameter (across).

Our moon is 2160 miles in diameter. Four moons would fit across the Earth's diameter. The moon is much smaller than the Earth. Fifty moons would fit inside our Earth. The moon appears to be the same size as the sun because it is much closer to us.

Experiment

Here is an experiment that explains why the moon seems so big.

1. Hold a penny 12" in front of your eyes. It appears large because it is close.
2. Now have a friend hold a penny up across the room. It appears small because it is far away.

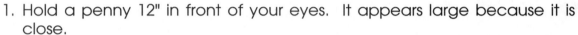

Phases of the Moon

The moon does not always appear the same. We call these changes **phases** of the moon.

Look at the sketch of the moon's phases. It is a 28-day cycle.

A **full** moon is a completely round circle of light. Fourteen days later we have the **new** moon. You see no light during a new moon.

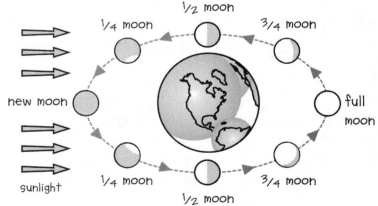

The Moon: Earth's Nearest Neighbor

Moon Phase Fun

Here is a way to "see" the moon phases for yourself.

1. Tape a light-colored ball to a pencil.
2. FInd a strong flashlight.
3. Darken the room and have a friend shine the flashlight towards you.
4. Hold the ball at arm's length above your head and face the light. The side of the ball facing you will be dark. This would be the new moon.
5. Turn your body so you are facing away from the light. The ball will be completely lit. This would be a full moon.
6. Turn your body slowly towards the light. You will see the different parts of the ball lit up like the moon phases.

25

Observing the Moon

Here is a way to track the moon phases. Observe the moon for 10 nights. Draw the moon's shape that you see each night.

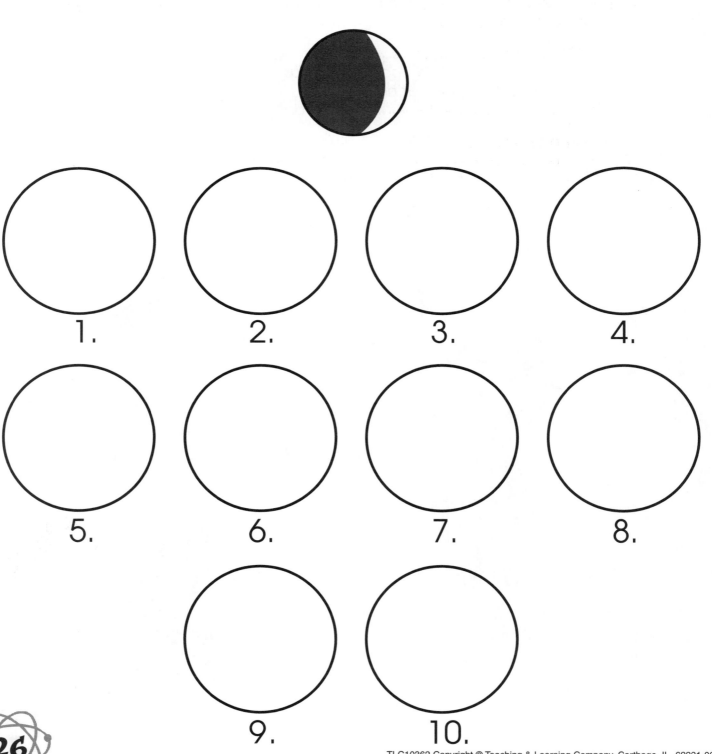

1.

2.

3.

4.

5.

6.

7.

8.

9.

10.

Name _____

Moon Poetry

The moon has been a favorite topic for songwriters and poets. Here is part of a famous poem called "The Moon" by Robert Louis Stevenson.

The squalling cat and the squeaking mouse,
The howling dog by the door of the house,
The bat that lies in bed at noon—
All love to be out by the light of the moon.

Turn your imagination loose. Look up at the moon tonight. Can you see faces or other objects? Write a poem about the moon in the circle.

Man on the Moon

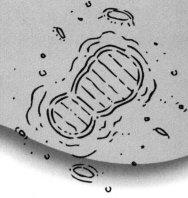

The Moon Is Not a Friendly Place

Living on Earth is easy. Living on the moon is not. Even getting to the moon is a problem. The moon is 240,000 miles from Earth. Both the Earth and the moon are in motion. It takes a lot of science to navigate to the moon.

Imagine that you are astronaut Neil Armstrong. He was the first man to set foot on the moon. Here are some of the problems to be faced:

1. There is no air on the moon to breathe.
2. There is no water on the moon to drink.
3. There are no plants or animals to use for food.
4. There are steep mountains to climb and deep craters to fall into.
5. Temperatures on the moon range from boiling to freezing.

There is one bit of good news. Gravity is much less on the moon. A person weighing 120 pounds on the Earth would only weigh 20 pounds on the moon. You could probably jump six feet high! You can't join Neil Armstrong on his moon walk, but you can salute the bravery of the 12 men who did walk on the moon.

Imagination Time
Astronauts left footprints on the moon. If you were an astronaut, what shape or symbol would you leave on the moon's surface?

I would leave the numbers 1 to 10 to show human intelligence.

How We Landed on the Moon

The date was July 20, 1969. Three astronauts had traveled to the moon in an Apollo spaceship. They were circling the moon. The pilot was Michael Collins. His job was to cruise around the moon. Neil Armstrong and Buzz Aldrin were to land on the moon. Armstrong and Aldrin used the **lunar module** to descend to the moon. Armstrong stepped onto the moon first. Then Aldrin joined him for the 22-hour visit on the moon. They planted the American flag. They collected 50 pounds of moon rocks to take back to Earth. Then the lunar module blasted off the moon, leaving the landing section behind. Lifting off was easy because the moon has very little gravity. The three astronauts rejoined above the moon. The lunar module was allowed to drift off into space. The rockets were fired and *Apollo 11* returned to Earth. There were five more Apollo missions to the moon. The last astronaut to step onto the moon was Gene Cernan. He left his footprint there in 1972. Footprints stay practically forever because there is no air or wind. There is no water or rain on the moon either. Wind and rain on Earth would soon wipe out any footprint here.

Packing for a Trip to the Moon

It is hard to decide what to take on a trip. Deciding what to take on a trip to the moon is even harder.

Here is a list of five items someone suggested for a moon trip. Only two of the items would be useful on the moon. Talk with your friends. Decide which two items are useful and which three are not. Write the reasons for your decisions below.

Items to Take to the Moon

box of matches, parachute, rope, life raft, oxygen

Items you will need and why.

1. _____
2. _____

Useless items and why.

1. _____
2. _____
3. _____

List five more items you could use on the moon.

1. _____
2. _____
3. _____
4. _____
5. _____

Is cat food on that list?

Man on the Moon

Craters on the Moon

The moon is full of deep holes called craters. Most of the craters are due to space objects smashing into the moon.

Craters differ in size. Some are less than 100 feet wide. The crater called **Copernicus** is almost 60 miles wide and two miles deep.

Copernicus was named after a famous astronomer.

Here is a way you can copy the moon's surface:

The Mud Bath

Add a small amount of water to an outdoor area. You want a thick, muddy surface. Throw some marbles into the mud. Throw some straight down and a few at an angle. Remove the marbles and admire the craters.

To-the-Moon Quiz

1. What would you weigh on the moon? (It would be one-sixth of your Earth weight.)

   _____

2. Which of these men did not walk on the moon?

   A. Armstrong   B. Copernicus   C. Collins   D. Aldrin

3. Which item would be useless on the moon?

   A. oxygen   B. water   C. candles   D. food

4. Why do footprints on the moon last forever?

   _____

   _____

5. Your spaceship travels 1000 miles per hour. How many hours would it take you to get to the moon?

   _____

The Solar System

Astronomy 7

How It All Began

No one knows for sure how our solar system began. Here is one popular explanation:

1. A huge cloud of gas and dust formed in space.
2. Gravity pulled the gas and dust toward the center.
3. The hot, dense center became the sun.
4. As the sun swirled around, it threw off masses of matter.
5. This matter clumped together to form the planets.

It is believed that the solar system is about five billion years old. It probably took billions of years for the planets to form.

Ancient people noticed that some objects in the night sky wandered through the star patterns. These were the planets moving across the sky. The word *planet* means "wanderer."

The solar system is very complex. It consists of the sun and nine planets. Many planets have moons circling them. There are also asteroids, bits of rock that never clumped together to form planets.

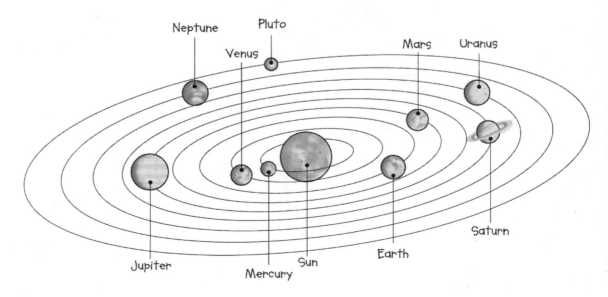

Name _____

The Solar System

Astronomy Heroes

There are sports heroes, soldier heroes, police and firefighter heroes. Meet these three astronomy heroes. Their ideas and experiments changed the way we think about the solar system.

Nicolaus Copernicus (1473-1543)
Before Copernicus, everyone believed the Earth was the center of the solar system. Copernicus proved that the sun is the center.

Galileo Galilei (1564-1642)
Galileo was the first man to study the heavens with a telescope. He observed the moon and planets. He discovered moons around other planets. His work proved that Copernicus was right.

Isaac Newton (1642-1727)
Newton was a math genius. He gave us laws that explain how the planets stay in orbit around the sun.

Wow! Ptolemy lived a long time ago!

Nicolaus Copernicus

Galileo Galilei

Isaac Newton

Below is a list of some other astronomy heroes. Try to learn something about one or more of them. Share what you learn with your friends.

Tycho Brahe	Benjamin Banneker	Albert Einstein
Robert Goddard	George Hale	Edmond Halley
William Herschel	Edwin Hubble	Percival Lowell
Ptolemy	Carl Sagan	Wernher Von Braun
Caroline Herschel	Maria Mitchell	Steven Hawking

Solar System Questions and Answers

Here are some questions and answers about our solar system. Some are answered with experiments.

1. How can I remember the names of all nine planets?

    Try this phrase that has all nine planets in their order from the sun.

    Mr. VEM J SUNP: Mercury, Venus, Earth Mars, Jupiter, Saturn, Uranus, Neptune, Pluto

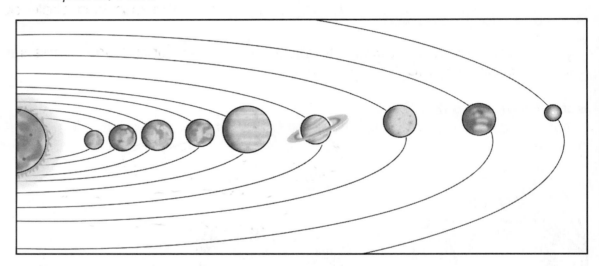

2. Planets look like stars in the sky. How can I tell the difference between a planet and a star?

    Planets wander through the star background. Stars twinkle as their distant light hits our air. Planet light is reflected light. It does not twinkle.

3. Why is the planet Mars a reddish color?

    The surface of Mars has many rocks that contain iron. The iron rusted to the red color.

    ### Experiment

    Let's try to rust iron. Find two iron nails. (Be sure they are made of iron, not coated to prevent rust.) Place them in a covered jar with a small amount of water in it. Wait a few days.

4. Why don't planets fly off into space?

    Isaac Newton explained this. Each planet is revolving or orbiting around the sun. What keeps the planets in orbit is the balance between the sun and the rotating force of each planet.

34

Balancing Gravity and the Force of Revolution

Here is an experiment to show how the two forces balance.

1. Punch a **small** hole in the bottom of a paper cup.
2. Push a four-foot string through the hole and outside of the cup.
3. Tie the string around the cup.
4. Hold the end of the string and rotate the cup in a circle above your head.

The cup is the Earth rotating in orbit. The string acts like the sun's gravity pulling inward on the Earth.

A Planet Hunt

The names of the nine planets appear in this word search, one time each. The word *sun* appears nine times. Find the words and circle them. Look across, down and diagonally.

```
V M Q M A R S Z L M
J E R P L U T O K L
U R N T H B Z N U S
P C H U S A T U R N
I U W S N H G A S N
T R S U N T Z Q N U
E Y N L R Z Y S U N
R U Y A S S U N S Z
S N E P T U N E R B
```

The Planets

 ## Facts About the Planets

There are nine planets, all different. Some are cold. Some are hot. Some are near. Some are far. Only our Earth seems able to support life. The planets are described below with a few important facts about each.

Mercury: Mercury is the closest planet to the sun. The temperature can reach 800°F. It is the second smallest planet. The very thin air around it is mainly helium gas. Mercury revolves around the sun in 88 Earth days.

Venus: Venus is very close to Earth in size. Venus is surrounded by clouds which reflect so much sunlight, it looks very bright. The air is mainly carbon dioxide. There is very little of the oxygen that we need. The temperature on Venus is hot enough to melt lead.

Mars: Mars is the next planet beyond Earth. It is smaller than Earth. Mars has many clouds and is windy. Two moons circle Mars. The temperature is about -70°F.

Jupiter: Jupiter is the largest planet. About 1300 Earths could fit inside it. Jupiter is the fourth brightest object in the sky. The air on Jupiter is mainly hydrogen and helium gas. Clouds form bands of color around Jupiter. It has a huge red spot, bigger than the Earth. The red spot is probably a storm drifting across Jupiter. Jupiter has 16 moons. The largest moon, called Ganymede, is larger than Mars.

Saturn: Saturn is the second largest planet. It has clouds that are mainly hydrogen and helium. The center of Saturn is solid rock. It is surrounded by thousands of rings made of chunks of ice and rocks. These rings make Saturn one of the most beautiful objects in the sky. It may have 18 moons.

Uranus: Uranus is so far away from Earth, it is rarely seen without a telescope. The air is made of hydrogen, helium and methane gas. The methane gas gives Uranus a bluish color. There are 17 moons circling Uranus.

Neptune: Neptune, about the same size as Uranus, also has clouds of methane gas. Neptune has eight moons and four thin rings.

Pluto: Pluto is the farthest planet. It is also one of the smallest. It is a ball of ice and rock with a temperature hundreds of degrees below zero. Pluto takes about 250 of our years to revolve around the sun.

Pluto

Neptune

Uranus

Saturn

Jupiter

Mars

Earth

Venus

Mercury

Sun

37

Planetary Review Quiz

Can you match each planet with the correct description?

_____ 1. Largest of the planets

_____ 2. The next planet beyond Earth

_____ 3. The farthest planet from the sun

_____ 4. Surrounded by large beautiful rings

_____ 5. The only planet with life

_____ 6. Almost the same size as the Earth

_____ 7. The nearest planet to the sun

_____ 8. Has hydrogen, helium and methane gas

_____ 9. Has eight moons and four thin rings

A. Mercury

B. Venus

C. Earth

D. Mars

E. Jupiter

F. Saturn

G. Uranus

H. Neptune

I. Pluto

AND IN A GALAXY FAR, FAR, AWAY...

Name _____

Planets for Sale

People who sell houses are called realtors. Imagine you are a planet realtor. You have nine planets for sale. Pick out a favorite one that you want to sell. Learn all you can about that planet. On another sheet of paper, prepare a full-page ad about your planet. Point out its good features. (If it is cold, you can keep food frozen. If it is hot, you can brag about barbecues.) Draw the planet below. List the good things on the planet you can brag about. Do not make a big deal about the planet's bad features.

Look in your local newspaper for ads about houses for sale. They will give you ideas about making your full-page planet sale ad.

Name _____

Planet Fun

You discover a new planet.

1. What will you name it? _____

2. Where will you place it in the solar system? _____
   _____

3. Write some interesting features of your new planet. _____
   _____
   _____
   _____

4. Your planet has no dirt or rocks. What is it made of? _____
   _____
   _____

How about a planet made of cat litter?

Brand-New Planet

Write your name here.

Planet Fun

Planet Size and Distance

It's fun to compare things. A basketball player is taller than a child. A bus is bigger than a car. Here is a planet comparison. Imagine that the sun is the size of a watermelon. The Earth would be a pea 1000 feet away. The distant planet Pluto would be a flea 8 miles away. Have students compare planets.

Chart 1: Planet Circle Size

Planet	Circle Diameter in Inches
1. Mercury	1
2. Venus	2$\frac{1}{2}$
3. Earth	2$\frac{1}{2}$
4. Mars	1$\frac{1}{2}$
5. Jupiter	28
6. Saturn	24
7. Uranus	10
8. Neptune	10
9. Pluto	1$\frac{1}{4}$

1. Draw planet circles. The sizes in chart 1 are fairly representational. They are in inches.

2. Cut the planet circles out of cardboard or heavy paper.

3. Label each planet. If possible, use red for Mars, blue for Earth and so on.

4. Measure off the planet distances from the sun. Do this in a long hall or outside.

5. Assign a student with a sunny disposition to be the sun. Assign a student to hold up each of the nine planet circles. Every planet person starts from the sun. Use chart 2 to measure the planet distances in feet. Mercury should stand 10 feet from the sun. Venus will be 18 feet, Mars 38 feet.

Chart 2: Planet Distances from Sun

Planet	Distance from Sun in Feet
1. Mercury	10
2. Venus	18
3. Earth	25
4. Mars	38
5. Jupiter	130
6. Saturn	240
7. Uranus	480
8. Neptune	750
9. Pluto	1000

You may not have enough room to measure the 1000 feet to Pluto. That is about three football fields.

Planet Fun

How Planets Orbit

All planets revolve in a path around the sun. The Earth takes 365 days or one year to revolve around the sun. Mercury revolves much faster around the sun. Its revolution or year takes only 88 of our Earth days. Mars is slower. It needs 687 of our Earth days to make a trip around the sun.

Why do planets stay in orbit around the sun instead of flying off into space? The answer is gravity. The sun's gravity balances their speed to keep them in orbit. Mercury is the closest planet to the sun. It is pulled by the greatest gravity. It has to move fast to keep from being drawn into the sun.

Experiment

Here is an experiment to show how the nearest planets revolve faster.

1. Attach a small rubber ball to three feet of string.
2. Run the string through a spool, and attach some weights to the opposite end. The combined weight of the items should be at least twice as heavy as the ball.
3. Go outside.
4. Hold the spool firmly and rotate the ball slowly, then rapidly. What did the heavy weight do?
5. Stop rotating the ball, and note how fast it spins as it is pulled inward.

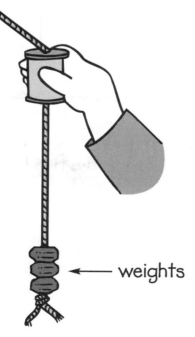

← weights

This can be related to the faster speed of the planets closest to the sun.

42

Create a Martian

Mars is not a friendly planet. Its surface is full of rocks, craters and volcanoes. Violent winds sweep dust across Mars. There are some clouds. There may be some frozen water at the poles of Mars. There are no plants or animals to use as food. Mars has no oxygen to breathe, though there may be some oxygen in the iron rocks.

What kind of creature could live on Mars?

Create a Martian.

1. Your creature can be made from tin cans, plastic jugs or bottles, milk cartons, doll parts, vegetables or old toys.

2. Do not use expensive parts. The creature must be made of common, simple materials.

3. Use your imagination to come up with something different.

4. Give it a name and share your Martian with your friends.

Try to create a creature that could survive on Mars. If Mars is cold, give your creature a fur coat.

Like mine!

Planet Scramble

The nine planets have had their letters scrambled. Can you unscramble them?

1. RAMS _____

2. URNTAS _____

3. HEART _____

4. CURYMER _____

5. PUNENET _____

6. TLUPO _____

7. NURSUA _____

8. SUNVE _____

9. TERIPUJ _____

I wonder if scrambled planets are as good as scrambled eggs?

The Stars

Astronomy 10

Look up in Wonder

Look up into the sky on any clear and dark night and you will see thousands of stars. There are billions more that you cannot see.

Experiment

To see the stars better, close your eyes for five minutes before looking up. This adjusts your eyes for seeing in the dark.

Where are all these stars during the day? Do they turn their lights out and sleep? They are still there in the sky. Sunlight is so bright you cannot see the dim stars.

When you look at a bright star, it may be 60 trillion miles away. The light entering your eye left the star 10 years ago.

How many stars are in the universe? You could never count them all. Astronomers think there may be as many stars as grains of sand on all the beaches on Earth.

How tall are you? How big are you compared to the Earth? How big are you compared to the entire universe? Don't you feel small?

A Galaxy of Stars

Most of the universe is empty space. Stars are usually found in clusters called **galaxies**. A galaxy is a mass of stars, dust and gas held together by gravity.

There are at least 10 billion galaxies in the universe. Each galaxy can contain billions of stars. Some galaxies are shaped like giant pinwheels with spiral arms. Our sun is just one star in our galaxy called the Milky Way. It is located in one of the spiral arms. Every star in every galaxy is in motion, all moving away from each other. Our sun and Earth are also moving out into space.

A Stargazer's Poem

People gaze at the beautiful stars with joy and wonder. Here is an old poem/song about the stars:

Twinkle, twinkle, little star,
How I wonder what you are
Up above the world so high
Like a diamond in the sky.
Twinkle, twinkle, little star,
How I wonder what you are.

Write your own short poem about the wonders of a starry night.

_____
Title

_____

_____

_____

_____

_____

_____

_____

_____

_____

_____

The Stars

Star Questions

Stars are hot, bright balls of gas. They get their energy by turning hydrogen gas into helium gas.

Here are some questions and answers about the stars.

1. Why do stars twinkle?

    Stars don't really twinkle. Light from a star travels through the Earth's air. The air causes the twinkle.

2. How old are the stars?

    Some stars were probably born 20 billion years ago. New stars are still being created out of gas and dust in space. Our sun may be five billion years old. It is expected to last another five billion years before burning up.

3. How far away are the stars?

    Stars all seem to be the same distance from the Earth, but they are all different distances. The nearest star to Earth is called Alpha Centauri. It is 25 trillion miles away.

4. How big are stars?

    Our sun is a bit less than a million miles in diameter. A thousand of our suns would fit across the diameter of some large stars.

5. Why do stars have different colors?

    Star color depends on the star's temperature. The hottest stars are blue. The coldest stars are red. Our star is yellow. It is not the hottest or the coldest star.

Experiment

You can get an idea of temperature and color by observing a candle.

Have an adult light a candle. Darken the room. Look at the candle. What different colors did you see in the flame?

Did you see a glow around the normal flame?

What color did you see at the bottom of the flame? That is the coldest part.

What color was at the top of the flame? That is the hottest part.

The Stars

Constellations

Constellations are imaginary star figures in the night sky. They may be a warrior, a bull or a crab.

Over a thousand years ago constellations were given names to help people memorize the sky.

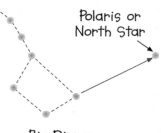

Polaris or North Star

Big Dipper

The Big Dipper is in the constellation called Ursa Major. This means "Big Bear."

Cassiopeia is a queen sitting on a throne. Orion is a warrior with a club.

Constellations appear to move as the Earth rotates and as the seasons change.

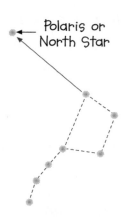

Polaris or North Star

Big Dipper rotated

Experiment

Here is a way for you to "find" and name your own constellation.

Get a saltshaker and some black paper. Sprinkle a tiny amount of salt all over the paper. Think of each salt grain as a star. Imagine a constellation shape. Draw it on the paper with a light-colored marker, connecting the grains of salt. Give it a name.

The Big Bear constellation forms a dipper in the sky. Look at the farthest two stars on the cup of the dipper. They point to the star Polaris. Polaris is called the North Star because it stays in the north at all times. It does not change position during the night like other stars.

The Big Dipper may rotate, but the two end stars always point to Polaris. When you find Polaris, you know where north is.

Constellation Viewer

Here is a way to show the constellations to your friends.

1. You'll need a paper towel cardboard tube and some black paper.

2. Use the tube to draw a circle on the black paper.

3. Cut a square around the circle about a 1/2" bigger.

4. Using a pin or thumbtack, punch sharp, clean holes in the circle. Start with holes that form a "W" as shown, for the constellation Cassiopeia.

5. Tape the circle on the end of the tube firmly.

6. Darken the room and view your constellation by looking through the tube toward a light source.

Try making the other constellations below.

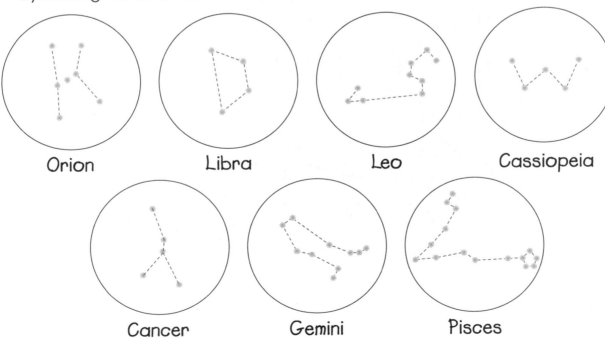

Orion   Libra   Leo   Cassiopeia

Cancer   Gemini   Pisces

Constellation Quiz

Match the words on the left with the correct answers on the right.

_____ 1. Polaris

_____ 2. Ursa Major

_____ 3. Cassiopeia

_____ 4. Star clusters

_____ 5. Star closest to our sun

_____ 6. Orion

A. Alpha Centauri

B. Galaxies

C. North Star

D. Queen on throne

E. Big Bear

F. Warrior with a club

TLC10362 Copyright © Teaching & Learning Company, Carthage, IL 62321-0010

Astrology

What Is Astrology?

Astrology goes back thousands of years. Astrologers believe that they can help you live your life.

Millions of people believe in and enjoy astrology. For some it provides a daily guide to life. For others it is a way of predicting their future.

Astrology is based upon the lineup of the sun and planets when you were born. Most scientists reject astrology. They say astrology predictions should not be taken too seriously.

The Friendly Zodiac

The Earth moves yearly through a pattern of constellations. The pattern has been known since ancient times as the **zodiac**.

Some zodiac signs are Leo (the lion), Taurus (the bull), Pisces (the fish) and Scorpio (the scorpion). They are related to your birthday. They supposedly tell how the stars and planets were lined up when you were born.

The 12 signs are associated with the four seasons. Find your sign on the list on the following page.

Examples: If you were born between March 21 and April 20, your sign is Aries. If you were born between December 22 and January 20, your sign is Capricorn.

March 21	Aries
April 20	Taurus
May 21	Gemini
June 22	Cancer
July 23	Leo
August 23	Virgo
September 23	Libra
October 24	Scorpio
November 22	Saggitarius
December 22	Capricorn
January 20	Aquarius
February 19	Pisces

I hope my sign is Leo the Lion!

Zodiac Signs

Each zodiac sign has a name and symbol.

Aquarius (water-carrier)

Pisces (fishes)

Aries (ram)

Taurus (bull)

Gemini (twins)

Cancer (crab)

Leo (lion)

Virgo (virgin)

Libra (balance)

Scorpio (scorpion)

Sagittarius (archer)

Capricornus (horned goat)

 Horoscopes

Horoscopes are daily predictions based on your zodiac sign. They are printed in most newspapers.

Here are some typical horoscopes found in a newspaper:

Leo (July and August): Wear different clothes. Change your hairstyle.

Aquarius (January and February): You will be complimented on your intelligence.

Pisces (February and March): Your major wish will come true.

Look up your horoscope in the newspaper. Compare it with a friend's horoscope. Enjoy them, but don't take them too seriously.

Building a Sextant

A Sextant

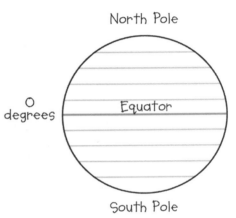

A **sextant** is an instrument used by sailors. It helps them find where they are, even in the middle of an ocean. It uses a telescope to locate the position of the North Star.

Here is how the sextant works. The Earth is divided into imaginary numbers called **latitude**. The equator is 0 latitude. Knowing the latitude helps you know how far above or below the equator you are.

North Pole

O degrees

Equator

South Pole

The North Star is the only star that is stationary (does not move) in the sky. A sextant measures how high the North Star is above the horizon. The North Star's height is also the latitude.

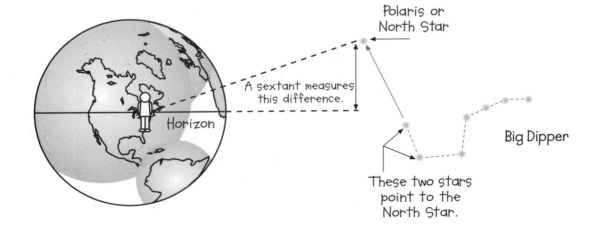

Polaris or North Star

A sextant measures this difference.

Horizon

Big Dipper

These two stars point to the North Star.

Name _____

How to Build a Sextant

1. Make a copy of the protractor below. A protractor is used in math to measure angles.

2. You'll need some thick cardboard, a large diameter drinking straw, a large paper clip, some string and tape.

3. Cut out your copy of the protractor.

4. Tape it to a slightly larger piece of cardboard.

5. Punch a hole where shown in the sketch and place one end of a 6" string through the hole. Tape it on the back of the cardboard.

6. Tie the paper clip to the other end of the string. The clip will act as a weight.

7. Mount a section of the large straw as shown in the sketch. The straw should stick out 1" on both sides.

8. Cut a 1" square of cardboard.

9. Cut out a small hole, as shown, the size of the straw.

10. Mount the cardboard circle on the left end of the straw. You may need to tape it on. This is your light shield to keep your eye focused through the straw.

11. Look through the straw at any high object. The string will move to some number on the protractor. These numbers are angles. You're ready to use your sextant. **_Do not look at the sun!_**

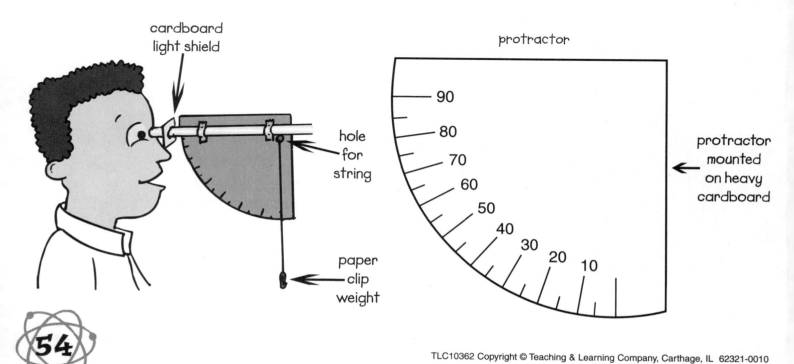

cardboard
light shield

hole
for
string

paper
clip
weight

protractor

90
80
70
60
50
40
30
20
10

protractor
mounted
on heavy
cardboard

Building a Sextant

The Sextant at Work

Have a friend read the angle where the string falls.

Here are some outdoor objects to measure with your sextant. You may find better outside objects in your area.

Example: The top of a small tree 20 degrees

1. Top of a tall tree _____ degrees
2. Top of a chimney _____ degrees
3. Top of a light pole _____ degrees
4. Top of a flagpole _____ degrees

Fun Challenge

Release a helium-filled balloon and take sextant measurements every minute.

Here are some night uses for your sextant.

1. Height of the moon early in the evening _____ degrees
2. Height of the moon late in the evening _____ degrees
3. Height of the North Star early in the evening _____ degrees
4. Height of the North Star late in the evening _____ degrees

Caution!
Do not use the sextant to look at the sun.

Polaris or
North Star

Big Dipper

Super Sextant Challenge

Could you build a better sextant? Think of a substitute for the small straw. Make the protractor bigger and more colorful or use a real protractor. How about a better string or weight? Make your super sextant at home, then bring it to class to share with your friends.

Sunlight

Sir Isaac Newton invented the prism to help him study sunlight.

We Need Sunlight

Our sun is 93 million miles away. The light from the sun travels at the speed of 186,000 miles a second. Even at that speed it takes sunlight almost eight minutes to reach the Earth.

Sunlight is a form of energy that can travel through empty space. We can see sunlight and feel its warmth.

We see objects because sunlight bounces off them. Our Earth is kept warm by it. Sunlight is needed to help plants make food. The energy in oil and coal is really stored sunlight.

Sunlight looks "white" to our eyes, but it is really a mixture of all the colors in the rainbow.

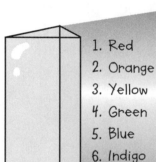

1. Red
2. Orange
3. Yellow
4. Green
5. Blue
6. Indigo
7. Violet

Study the drawing. It shows how a glass prism can turn sunlight into a rainbow.

Experiment

Here is a way to make your own rainbow. You will need a strong flashlight, black tape, a white card and a glass of water.

1. Use the black tape to create a 1/4" slit on the face of the flashlight as shown.
2. Place the glass of water on the edge of a chair.
3. Place the white card right below the chair.
4. Darken the room.
5. Adjust the flashlight beam so it angles through the glass of water as shown.
6. Adjust the position of the white card on the floor so it is centered on the rainbow that forms.
7. List the colors in the order you see them.

Sunlight

Why the Sky Is Blue

The sky looks blue on a clear day. Why should the sky look blue when sunlight has all the rainbow colors?

The answer is the dust in our air. Dust tends to "spread" out mainly blue light. Dust doesn't spread out other colors as much.

Experiment

Here is an experiment to show why the sky is blue. You'll need a tall glass, a strong flashlight and some nonfat milk.

1. Fill the glass three-fourths full of water.

2. Add a few drops of milk to act as dust. Stir the water and milk.

3. Darken the room. Shine the light straight down on the water and milk as shown.

4. Look at the jar from the side. You should see a bluish tinge to the liquid.

I'll clean it up when you're done.

57

Eclipses: Shadows in the Sky

Lunar Eclipse

sun

Earth   moon

moon moves behind Earth

You have seen shadows. Some are beautiful; some are scary. The Earth and the moon can also cast shadows.

The sun, Earth and moon are all in motion. The Earth revolves around the sun. The moon revolves around the Earth. Sometimes they line up and cast a shadow.

A lunar (moon) eclipse occurs when the moon moves into the Earth's shadow. A lunar eclipse can last for over an hour.

Solar Eclipse

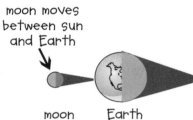

moon moves between sun and Earth

sun

moon   Earth

A solar (sun) eclipse occurs when the moon is between the Earth and the sun. The moon's shadow falls on the Earth. A solar eclipse can last seven minutes. Birds, other animals and even plants can be fooled into thinking it is night.

Caution! Do not use the sextant to look at the sun.

Shadow Fun

It is fun to make shadow figures with your hands. Try the animal shadows below.

Making Your Own Eclipse

Here is a way to demonstrate solar and lunar eclipses. You will need a strong flashlight, a basketball and a tennis ball.

1. Darken the room.

2. Have someone be the sun and hold the flashlight. Have another person hold the basketball and be the Earth and a third person hold the tennis ball and be the moon.

3. Arrange the light and balls (with the basketball between the light and the tennis ball) as shown for a lunar eclipse. You may have to adjust the light and ball distances. Note the Earth's shadow on the moon.

4. Arrange the light and balls (with the tennis ball between the light and the basketball) for a solar eclipse as shown. Adjust the distances as needed.

Lunar Eclipse

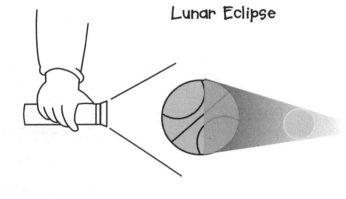

Eclipses only happen when the sun, Earth and moon are lined up just right. Most of the time they do not line up for an eclipse. Newspapers and television usually tell when and where eclipses will happen.

Solar Eclipse

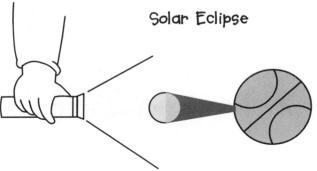

Gravity

Explaining Gravity

We would fly off the Earth without gravity. The Earth would leave the sun and drift into space without gravity.

What is gravity? No one has ever seen it or touched it. Nothing stops gravity. It is found on the tops of mountains and in the deepest mines.

The truth is, we don't really know how gravity works. All we know is that it pulls things down to Earth. Just what does the pulling is a mystery.

There is a place where you can escape gravity. Astronauts orbiting in space are weightless. They float around without effort. The lack of gravity causes some problems. Being weightless makes for some very interesting experiments.

Imagination Time
You are now an astronaut. What experiment would you like to try in a weightless spaceship? Gravity is both helpful and a problem on Earth. It fights you when you try to lift heavy objects. Imagine you have been given a "magic" marker to remove gravity. How would you use your anti-gravity marker?

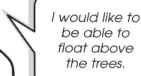

I would like to be able to float above the trees.

60

Name _____

Gravity Changes

The pull of gravity is not always the same. The Earth is not exactly round. It bulges at the equator. It is smaller at the poles.

If Allie lived in New York and weighed 60 pounds, she would weigh slightly less at the equator. She would weigh slightly more at the North and South Poles. She would only weigh 15 pounds if she were 8000 miles above the Earth.

Let's send CD to the moon. The moon is much smaller than the Earth. It only has one-sixth of the Earth's gravity. If CD weighed 72 pounds on Earth, he would only weigh 12 pounds on the moon. CD can jump two feet high on Earth. He could jump twice that high on the moon. CD could throw a football over 100 yards on the moon and lift a 300-pound weight.

CD's mom weighs 100 pounds on Earth. What would she weigh on other planets? To find out, use the planet weight table at the right. Multiply Mom's weight by the gravity number.

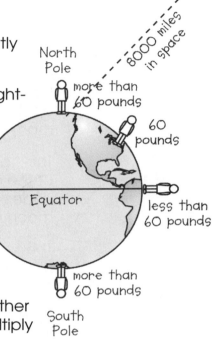

Example: Mars is 0.38 times 100 = 38 pounds.

1. Mom's weight on Mercury is _____ pounds.
2. Mom's weight on Venus is _____ pounds.
3. Mom's weight on Jupiter is _____ pounds.
4. Mom's weight on Saturn is _____ pounds.
5. Mom's weight on Uranus is _____ pounds.

Planet	Grav. No.
Mercury	0.38
Venus	0.86
Jupiter	2.87
Saturn	1.32
Uranus	0.93

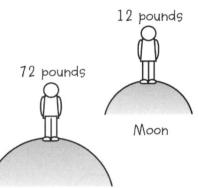

Name _____

Gravity and Tides

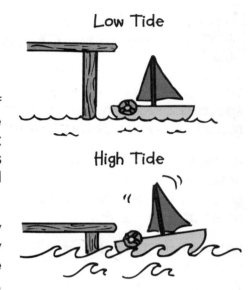

Low Tide

High Tide

If you live near an ocean, you are aware of **tides**. Tides are bulges in the level of the ocean. These bulges occur about every six hours. There are two high and two low tides each day. The water level can rise and fall many feet.

The tides are caused mainly by the gravity of the moon. Tides are really waves directly under the moon. The waves follow the moon in the monthly orbit around the Earth.

The sun also affects tides. The sun has much more gravity than the moon, but it is much farther away. The sun's gravity effect is about half that of the moon.

Study the drawing at the left. It shows the moon raising the ocean beneath it to cause a high tide. There is also a smaller high tide on the opposite side of the Earth. The moon's gravity is pulling the Earth away from the water.

Moon

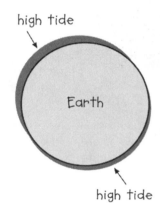

high tide

Earth

high tide

Experiment

This experiment will help you understand tides. Magnetism will be substituted for gravity. You'll need a magnet, some steel washers and an envelope.

1. Place the washers inside the envelope as shown.
2. Seal the envelope.
3. Tape the envelope to a table.
4. Slowly move the magnet over the envelope. It should be close but not touching the envelope.
5. Observe the envelope (the ocean) bulge up as the magnet (the moon's gravity) passes by.

62

Fooling Gravity

Sometimes you can arrange common objects to "fool" gravity. Look at the examples below. You are really changing the center of gravity. Try to fool gravity by doing one or more of these experiments.

Isn't science fun?

Answer Key

Space Quiz, page 12

1. false   5. false
2. false   6. true
3. false   7. false
4. true   8. true

Earth Friendly Quiz, page 18

1. The Earth rotates on its axis and revolves around the sun.
2. gravity
3. A. water, B. heat, C. air, D. food, E. energy
4. universe, galaxy, solar system, Earth, moon
5. Answers will vary.

Sun Fun, page 19

1. hot   3. big
2. far   4. old

Sunny Quiz, page 22

1. D   5. F
2. C   6. E
3. B   7. A
4. G

Packing for a Trip to the Moon, page 29

Need rope and oxygen. Don't need matches, parachute or life raft.

To-the-Moon Quiz, page 31

1. Answers will vary.
2. B and C
3. C
4. There is no air or wind on the moon.
5. 240 hours or 10 days

A Planet Hunt, page 36

```
V M Q M A R S Z L M
J E R P L U T O K L
U R N T H B Z N U S
P C H U S A T U R N
I U W S S N H G A S
T R S U N T Z Q N U
E Y N L R Z Y S U N
R U Y A S S U N S Z
S N E P T U N E R B
```

Planetary Review Quiz, page 38

1. E   6. B
2. D   7. A
3. I   8. G
4. F   9. H
5. C

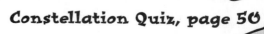

Planet Scramble, page 44

1. Mars   6. Pluto
2. Saturn   7. Uranus
3. Earth   8. Venus
4. Mercury   9. Jupiter
5. Neptune

Constellation Quiz, page 50

1. C   4. B
2. E   5. A
3. D   6. F

64

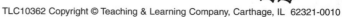